MORE PRAISE FOR *ZIRCONIUM ASH*

"Freeway poems, a driver's night soliloquies refracting city lights through gleaming obsidian glass, '78 on the 90 & searching for my abuelito's voice'——glancing backwards once in a while, jimmy vega is glimpsed in the rearview mirror, our gaze crosses his. These freeways loop through dreams and regrets, memories and grief. '95 on the 105'—we're driving through the dark with headlights switched off—a Thomas Guide abandoned under the seat after Google maps appeared on everyone's phone, revised here as the jimmy vega Guide. You'll recognize the freeways at night and the signs. You'll recognize this inner city. In these poems L.A. is always on fire."
—SESSHU FOSTER, author of *ELADATL: A History of the East Los Angeles Dirigible Air Transport Lines*

"There is an incandescent calm at the core of jimmy vega's tumbling, raging, epic freeway lyrics. The poems map Los Angeles, a 'city rot with ghosts,' family history, as well as the crimes of the U.S. government. I feel the tendril traces of Wanda Coleman here, where city pavement is as much a canvas for what is spilled, as these pages are for capturing grief, anger, despair. These poems keen and are anthem—I wish I had this book to keep me company during my formative years living in LA."
—DIANA KHOI NGUYEN, author of *Root Fractures*

"From the stunning ars-poetica-as-freeway opener to the sleeping angel 'on blue / graphite pavement' of its penultimate lines, *zirconium ash* performs an exorcism of the self, a reckoning of civic amnesia, a 'five-car collision' of things ever on the verge of being lost to the stupor of Los Angeles, a 'city persimmon in afterglow.' As this rebellion of the senses gives way to shades of marigold, wildfire, and carbon monoxide, jimmy vega encounters his own suffering and arrested breath in that of family separations, police brutality, lethal air-borne elements, and concussive, algorithmic low-theory deliriums, drawing us ever closer and in concert with these vatic, expansive poems, such that 'i can almost taste the snare of my own language.'" —ROBERTO TEJADA, author of *Carbonate of Copper*

"To read jimmy vega's elegiac, anguished, and expansive poems is to experience an unleashing of ritualistic force that, at times, rushes at 78 (or 95) mph and, at others, stops on a dime before a surprising voltaic turn. This is a poetry of ghosts, of angels, of vulnerable bodyminds—all seasoned with the flavor of 'iron & ash / from burning los angeles.' vega practices—and preaches—a Dionysian formalism that rejects the oppressive sun of Apollo. This is why *ash*—that which remains after the fire, that which teeters on the brink of existence and an ecstatic scattering of annihilation—is such a potent figure in this book. As for *zirconium*: by some accounts, the word comes from the Arabic word 'zargon,' which means 'gold-like.' *zirconium ash* revels, then, and reveals itself in a sometimes jubilant and sometimes jarred jargon that is more shiningly potent and subversively cinderous than Wallace Stevens' 'gold flourisher': 'if you show / me your parasitic apathy, i'll show you / the zirconium ash in my brain.' When 'empire leaves [us] gasping' and when we're 'driving towards a vanishing ecosystem,' every day is the day of the dead; and that, vega insists, is cause for lyric celebration even if such lyricism is articulated through a 'flutter of iambic / convulsions,' through a 'song of bleeding throats.'" —MICHAEL LEONG, author of *Contested Records: The Turn to Documents in Contemporary North American Poetry*

"jimmy vega's poignant *zirconium ash* brings us to a California only a poet knows how to describe. As vega puts deftly and concretely: 'This is not an allegory—this is another freeway poem.' But 'another' is modest here because of how the freeway measures life so fully: how it courses through these pages only in the way vega can move. His poetry, like the freeway, traverses through the 'goddamn' world or 'lake' and gets us to think about the work of the poet right now: 'about locking myself in stanzas & calling it a closet—a tiny room this is a poem about cages around a goddamn lake where do you put the houseless when you take away their less—when you un-shelter

their home?' The poems imprint themselves in the 'less' and inhabit all the more with which we need to think, encapsulating an essential vernacular and wit we desperately yearn for in this very moment."
—PRAGEETA SHARMA, author of *Grief Sequence*

"*zirconium ash* is a hole-punched sheaf of watch reports from vigils at the bedsides of the dead and dying; thus, everyone everywhere, though especially Los Angeles. jimmy vega perches there red-eyed and teeth uncollected as the ailing breathe in 'skid row piss cigarette / freeway carcass splat ash'—then, breathed out as cempasúchtil ash, the book's incremental refrain and evidence of ecological, sociopolitical, and personal fortunes 'in graveyard motion.' Ashes, ashes, we all crawl down the 710, the 5, the 91, these the rivers vega's known, charred under the same 'endless sun' that's surveilled Herrera, Coleman, Bukowski, and 150 years of riots. The same sun stink-eyeing everyone everywhere now. With these delirious yet lucid poems, vega stands in that light and he doesn't even squint."
—DOUGLAS KEARNEY, author of *I Imagine I Been Science Fiction Always*

"jimmy vega's Los Angeles is a freeway necropolis, where the living and the dead shoot past each other at high speeds, mingling voices— and flesh. I don't know if I've encountered poetry that engages the experience of the freeway with this uncompromising intensity—vega's asphalt corridors are thrilling, ghostly, and all too real. In creating this poetry vega sings us—with gritty Angeleño lyricism—into a basic lived reality of LA: that a few minutes from any given place down a roaring tube of concrete strangers are hurtling alongside each other in metal boxes at 80 miles an hour, each inside the emotional enormity of their cluttered lives, each inches from death, each themselves filled with their own ghosts. He also does not spare us this basic truth, that every day, someone among them will not make it home."
—ANTHONY MCCANN, author of *I am the dead, who, you take care of me*

WHAT BOOKS PRESS

AN IMPRINT OF

THE GLASS TABLE

COLLECTIVE

LOS ANGELES

zirconium ash

zirconium ash

poems

jimmy vega

WHAT
BOOKS
PRESS

LOS ANGELES

Library of Congress Cataloging-in-Publication Data

Names: vega, jimmy, 1990- author
Title: Zirconium ash : poems / jimmy vega.
Description: Los Angeles : What Books Press, 2025. | Summary: "Centered
    around loss and death of individuals, relationships, and ways of
    communicating, the poems of zirconium ash drive at intensified high
    speed, physically and psychically mapping the geography of the city of
    Los Angeles. Weaving and zigzagging, mingling grief, sorrow, and lament,
    the poems haunt and are haunted by the living and dead. The culture of
    the city and family history often blur in these poems, which can feel in
    conversation with themselves as well as others-fragmented ghost
    narratives that lyrically confront history, poetics, and the crimes and
    unjust actions of government"-- Provided by publisher.
Identifiers: LCCN 2025033009 | ISBN 9798990014992 paperback
Subjects: LCGFT: Poetry
Classification: LCC PS3622.E427 Z57 2025
LC record available at https://lccn.loc.gov/2025033009

Front cover: Gronk, *Untitled*, mixed media on paper, 2024

Back cover: *jimmy vega, Poet, 2023* from *Chicano Male Unbonded series*
© 2023, Harry Gamboa Jr.

Book design by ash good, www.ashgood.com

What Books Press
363 South Topanga Canyon Boulevard
Topanga, CA 90290

WHATBOOKSPRESS.COM

for Maggie, Jaime, Omar, Angel, & Ivan Vega
for Gladys Quintero

en memoria de

Elisa Garibay Romero De Vega (1929-2021)

y

Francisco Magaña (1942-2021)

CONTENTS

SOMETIMES, I WISH I COULD FAX THIS TO YOU

CEMPASÚCHTIL ASH

We died prodigiously; it hurt awhile
But left a certain quiet in our eyes.

—Jack Spicer

ANOTHER FREEWAY POEM—
AN ARS POETICA
WRITTEN NEAR THE 710

I.

this is another freeway poem—

this is another highway poem
      this is another poem about a road—

                  this is a poem about mothers separated
                        from their children by ice
                  this is a poem about cages—about mothers
                        locked in cages—about fathers locked in cages—
                              about parents locked in cages
                        about children locked in cages—

about locking myself in stanzas & calling it a closet—a tiny room

            this is a poem about cages around a goddamn lake
where do you put the houseless when you take away their less—
      when you un-shelter their home?

            this is a poem about mothers locked inside 6:00 a.m.
            closing their sleep lids with lights on in
                  adelanto, california—carefully holding their
                  children inside their cornea

2.

this is another poem about rushing home

my brother tells me—*drive safe*
        zero traffic—78 on the 90 & searching for my abuelito's voice
                as if wiping my mother's tears would break-light-red anguish

                          this is another freeway poem
                        another poem about mothers
                                losing fathers

        my father—rushing towards stone streets or else michoacán avenidas
his mother won't recall his face most days—
      & the day she left him—stained his dream tears puddled salt wounds
                   his face child slack & lost

this is another freeway poem
another poem about fathers
        losing mothers

    this is a poem about mothers losing their children
                      for selling loose cigarettes

this is a poem about nicotine-drenched roads
        this is a poem about crying for a mother into pavement
                this is a poem about murder for twenty dollars—news media
upset at acab cardboard signs & bricks
                        shattering corporate wilshire & fairfax

            this is a poem about cops tear gassing us & coloring
                              our iris blood red

3.

this is another poem about car crashes bruising my ribs
until i understood what anaphora meant

because pain is everything, ~~because pain is everything,~~
because pain is everything, ~~because pain is everything,~~
because pain is everything, ~~because pain is everything,~~
because i keep trying to shake your fingertips off my aphasia—

this is another poem about black & brown kids knowing
alliteration through the sound of bullets ringing
in the cities of lynwood, watts, & compton, so we scribble strophes on the soles
of our mother's feet & we color tanka on traffic signs in pastel acrylics

this is another freeway poem silenced not by carbon dioxide
but by asphyxiation learning refrain while kissing concrete—please—
i can't breathe
i can't breathe
i can't breathe
(   )
(   )

this is a poem about joseph crashing inside his mother's arms before
her lungs collapse

her body vanishing—

i can hear her voice—bioluminescent withering, dissipating in ocean breath

joseph tells me he'd *eat her cancer* if he could   a beautiful drowning
        crashing waves near the south bay—catatonic daydreams past dizzy
1:10 a.m. torrance streets gray & phosphorous—skeletal cavity driving towards
half brightness of her sleep

clouded graphite bereavement
        traffic light glare

                        —this is not an allegory—this is another freeway poem

4.

alexey tells me my pain is temporary
                          as if i'm not suffering upon suffering upon suffering

                                        so i swallow antistrophes—

on mornings when i hear my abuelito's
voice inside chalino sánchez lyrics
because pain is everything

his laugh lost inside lynwood avenues
because pain is everything

reverberating voice tucked inside
my optic nerve   i can see it if i'm quiet
because pain is everything

                who am i hurting writing this
                          is this my diaphanous death

& the scrawl blasted on freeway concrete is poetry, same way the light that
        glares on raw sewage in the flower district is poetry, same way food
        trucks appear as stanzas on olympic or la brea, that too, is poetry,
        same way a chain-link fence can't keep us out is poetry, same way
        the angel on broadway & 7th, shirtless, open feet to the ground,
        singing street songs is poetry

rearrange this line abab to feel something
              call it a midnight boulevard elegy, wrap it in neon plastic

this is a poem about collapse—
              abecedarius;
                    actually briefly
                          chasing daydreams
                                escaping finality

pirouetting on the 110 to my friends
        forecast liminal brightness tucked
              inside shadow-play southbound & lost

                          los angeles is a burning palm tree—
                          & i keep choking on raining soot

        i can't breathe in a city rot with ghosts

I'D GIVE A LOT OF EVERYTHING
TO SIT IN YOUR SUFFERING

i wanna be unsubscribed from my digital vertigo of transient escalator rendezvous

when do we realize that our parents
are not only the ghost light inside us but smell

after rain, a homeward frontier etched in cracked
asphalt—i taste an emptiness that scratches the

god in my throat when i remember that i once
hurt you—i said i taste an emptiness that scratches

the god in my iris when i recall how much i've lost
you—los angeles only feels this cute with you

new romantic hood skyline pigeon flutter concrete
where else—only except to smell the world burning

i am no longer a list of attachments

i am no longer a list of attachments
a sensory amalgamation as combustion
neurosis / i am my mother's quiet prayer
transient flicker brief as causality, hazy
amber videotape hue, unexcavated mem-
ory / i am the formal cause of an un-

found poem, weightless & yearning
in rimbaudian solitude / now that i am
in love & no longer a poet / instead

hummingbird singing my grand-
mother's secrets, one whose ashes

are kept in non-cobwebbed ancient church
archival box revolution / i keep thinking
about who you'd be if i'd never left / how
the desert can't hold you or how all flowers
beg for rain / i keep reading in the dark

to hide my lizard brain by licking
my own wounds / if pain is everything—
my tongue becomes my sacrificial ofrenda /
yearning to meet you within golden hum

there is a streetlight lost inside all of us
how else could we radiate past midnight

if you've ever been followed inside
fluorescent isles of a convenience store
raise your hand & repeat after me when
my grandmother died i lost a lot of every-
thing but not just anything, one who'd
pray for me rushing towards slate streets

i hear her voice in the action
of photosynthesis in the liminality of sleep
lids chasing moon cycles, elegiac & round &
cylindrical in a way that carries how
else did i ever fall asleep without you holding
my hand & now that i'm in love
& no longer a poet the ending is refrain

we go to washington next week

language it seems
      does not snake

a cross street with-
      out name dimly lingers

never have i ever smiled
      catching gaze of a monet

inside a dentist office pressure
crystalizes into plastic ocean saw

dust & i am no longer fun no longer
a myopic twinkle—a familiar harm-

ony, a long wavering sentimentality

—this is what they call a poem in semiotics // /

in the morning, you say a word like oscillating

voicemail i ching

i leave the i ching in the car

      you ask   & i listen

some loves are ghosts

      you ask   & i carry three coins

who do you wish you could call

      a voicemail is a letter in voice—

war is never over   in my pocket

      divinity ///

i reach for the i ching

            & i ask

— —

i leave the i ching closed

      overflowing my mind

some transmissions are more sacred

      yellow flower   gaped

mouth   there is divinity in spit

an angel on the exit of the 90 sits

      soaks sun, closed eyes

            gazing at me

an insect leaves this realm & i hear

         a popping sound

quiet whisper, glorious & hitherto rever-

berating ///   divinity in sacrifice

— —

ephemeral clashing bird song

      serene & ubiquitous

tell me about god cause i've almost forgotten

      as you milk sunrise into oblivion

feed every hungry atom of my body

      way a sleepy kiss murmurs

         forget-me-nots

& i listen—

— —

i dream the i ching on my freeway bed

       pass the overpass pass my tortured

darlings   you ask   & i listen

some loves are sentences that keep repeating,

       —a comma splice hidden as run-on

cultivate technologies   an ofrenda

       is archive   is praxis

a folded ladder inside a gallery in shadow

a voicemail is letter   is voice

       i'd give a lot of everything to sit

       in your suffering   in your thirst

a voicemail is a letter   often unopened

       archival transubstantiation breath

melting inside your *fade into you* cosmic day-

dreaming   like the eudaimonia found intensely

       in staring into sunset-mirrored-ocean

       through a lens of glass-polymer

my own déjà vu revisiting me
my own déjà vu revisiting me
my own déjà vu revisiting me

                        you ask...

& i listen—

persimmons

sticky fingers prickling persimmons
        marigold like crinkled crackling
        leaves on pavement   or blood
on terracotta   in my grandmother's
        cornea   one with golden
hair now graphite   she smiles
at me from afar   from across lawns
        on abbott rd   & i think of my
cousin jorge   who was secuestrado
by men with masks or crooked teeth
                        in michoacán streets summer
                                & stone

—did he cry when he was hungry?
   did they bust his lip with semiautomatics
                        & did he pray for my madrina lupe's
arms around him—4:16 a.m. cold like
        gray or wet clay in the arroyo
while sticky fingers clenched
                for god or blood—
pupils christen in blindfold
        crawling over gravel & glass
like kissing ground in service
        of forgiveness   or darkness

a woman walks on beethoven st
        cradling cempasúchtil flowers &
frowns at me as i taste iron & ash
from burning los angeles

sunlight hitting
glass color of persimmons &
i wonder if jorge tasted tierra or if he just
quivered his sticky fingers reaching
for another cigarette—6:14 a.m. cold
like silent streets or pavement
in the city he calls patria—

poem about my uncle

after Jose Hernandez Diaz

someone walks into the neighborhood liquor mentioning the total collapse
of civilization, sadden, recalling my notes on humanism, i reach for my dusky
scratch wrinkle of a gag—i thought i'd seen my uncle one day on my way to
work, down venice blvd crowning a dark baseball cap. sometimes i try holding
my grief in the palm of my hands & sometimes i lose my focus because even
sustenance can terrain. in that reverberating glimmer it was almost as if my uncle
was casually providing his salutations to the not yet dead through nonverbal
clairvoyance, way a blue jay sparkles its tongue to show you light, way my father
caressed my uncle's feet as he was dying;

there are moments we call collapse between lines we say before a mirror—either
static near black reflective or other dark brown mustard turf. i wonder when
exactly i had realized i was too late for lucid goodbyes, hood asphalt quiet sound.
i never see my cousins save to bear their suffer—

tonight, i cannot locate the little zen pocketbook of folk tales & allegories my
aristotelian teacher would read, like the koan about a strawberry by the cliff side.
if you listen closely the humming rarely stutters, an acknowledgment of presence,
like the last time i saw my uncle, he was already memory i could not cling to,
ghetto bird quiet display of suffering, how lonesome death, even with a nurse by
your side—i try telling you i can't be my own witness to the cosmic slow dance,

even if the constant surveillance does induce ocular headaches, in such a way
that privacy is no longer private nor free, in such a way that i ache before
afternoon catnaps, in such a way that empire leaves me gasping,

living near or living parallel or sleeping next to freeways is sociopolitical
redlining, don't kid yourself, we're well past savoir faire by this line. in that haze
of momentary flicker, my uncle, with his gaze, concentrating on asphalt was my
very own pareidolia…a stranger under the guise of my father's brother, one he
lost to microscopic or otherwise tumors nesting in his brain, smiling—

room 237

the last time i watched
     the shining on the big
screen we shared caramel
     corn & i lost the car keys
inside your coral reef smile

your eyes like shelley duvall's—
     glossy & silver like wet
algae on concrete, you still sniffle
when you cry as you pour
     redrum
on ice & i was *all work & no*
play makes jack a dull boy all
work & no play makes jack a
dull boy
     all work. no play. jack.

coastal freeway cold & catatonic
     65 on the 105 weak   night   quiet
& starless & ocean, what color
     were your dashboard lights inside
that yaris? black north face wind-
     breakers maybe in 68 degrees windless
spring nights, salt of your gray blue voice transient
ocean breeze on the tip of my tongue—
& you didn't flinch when jack nicholson
& blood appeared on screen

the last time i watched the shining
       on the big screen my voice was blood
red & you whispered
       darling, light of my life
as i ordered a medium root beer & your
retina quivered like dying jellyfish—
no one cared about the vanishing ecosystem then

listening to your playlist while driving made me feel like i was in your car again going around l.a.

—driving the 5, thinking of damian
      for no reason at all—i hold his surrender
          inside the back pocket of my iris

      ways he hurt himself to bury a deadname
          dark sleepy eye acquiesce shapeshifter

      —i miss the color of his grogginess—

      taiwanese night market rummaging for his
      mother's shadow in dizzy streets of burgundy
      bone broth warm salt & ash tucked in no light

i'd reach for the fishbone stuck in his throat

      if he'd let me

driving the 5, i scream—
      suffocate my goddamn self
      past griffith park thinking of damian
          for no reason at all—i hold his smile
          inside the trunk of my under-the-influence
          self-aware pity, mirrorless gaze haunts me

i wonder if i ever gave damian enough of my love

—my love, i hope you're okay in the bay
i hope you don't stumble around searching
for your keys in the morning
for no reason at all—i suffocate myself
only to recall october sunset embers
fire burnt mid-city late drives & swallowing
ash—probably could've died if i made
that right lane switch   heard your voice instead

i've been trying to find you inside a merwin poem

a later piece without punctuation

& it's the saddest ones who have the raspiest voices—
why'd you leave me in a city that is constantly burning

—driving the 5, whispering to myself
who's judas in all of this, thinking of damian
for no reason at all—i stroke my lament till
it becomes prayer or sacrilege fragment

are some of the old colors still there

i've been searching for you between quintessence & dusk

have you finally collected your teeth

collapsed lung

he lay in a hospital bed.
tethered to swelling pain
tangled in blue—
on machines casting sigils
shifting shadows
shattering sleep—
did you dream
melatonin dreams?
did you dream of me?
rhythmically twitching
flutter of iambic
convulsions
irises color
of undertone
half-tucked in bed
morphine kisses
staggered sighs
whimpers like mousetraps
hydrocodone half-smiles
stumbling eyes
sumatriptan somersaults
cold smell, like wet linoleum,
drowsiness like a flickering
streetlamp—monitoring
frayed breaths
pulsing heartbeat
keeping tabs
haphazardly harassed
by wires—

my brother,

he's getting an echo today

your boy's body, lanky,
16 years old, slipping into
crescendo whispers—
dreaming of phosphorescence

song of bleeding throats

los angeles is on fire

scorched streets toned
    in technicolor & rancid
        cempasúchtil ash. someone
    lights a cop car in flames

tear gas kisses my cornea tickles
    my throat like razor wire rattling
    my lungs & someone baptizes
    me in cool milk   my face drips...

    someone punches a cop & i make
        a wish—

hands outstretched—
    open palms—searching for god or
        loose cigarettes

*

i can't breathe on fairfax & 3rd
      i can't breathe with a fist down my throat
      i can't breathe with my face kissing
pavement—i can't breathe *in sleeper holds*
      i can't breathe in tobacco-stained roads
i can't breathe with a baton licking my spine
      i can't breathe with pepper spray coloring
my iris—i can't breathe when *we're choking*
on words like pig—i can't breathe when rubber
bullets hemorrhage my prefrontal lobe—i can't
breathe when i'm too busy coughing up a lung
      i can't breathe when my face is buried in tierra
i can't breathe cuando me amarran la lengua—
      i can't breathe, i can't breathe, i can't breathe
      (   )
      (   )

                          *

carbon monoxide tints the air green & someone
        holds an acab sign. i can smell burnt fingertips
reaching towards lit canisters. i can't breathe &
        it ain't the fucking face mask. someone says *the dumpsters*
in santa monica are a lot nicer than the ones in venice,
        the 405 southbound slack & slightly overcast. green
freeway signs scribbled in post semantics—i keep driving
        95 on the 405 before i reach inside my epidural hematoma
just to taste the fever of my city persimmon in afterglow

                    i can't breathe in los angeles

        my breath arrested   my voice cyanotic—

A FLOW OF ENERGY WHICH
IS NOT VISIBLE

five-car collision playlist:
a sonnet about freeways

i ask what you think of when you close your sleep lids,
as if drowning in mezcal was the same as tasting mercury
as if drowning in blood was the same shade of your iris
when an airbag kissed your face. angel tells me he still
sees shadow shades, break-light-red-lip-stains on the corner
of lemon & muffles silently inside my mother's arms—
trembling on highway pavement, concussion cruise control
while the exhaust burns & coral polyps hemorrhage like
crimson on porcelain, gums raw—*i cry not for myself*
as if a five-car collision isn't tethered to ocean sleep
as if sunsets weren't persimmon ash, carbon monoxide
splotches as if monet envisioned ozone depletion, deciding
to vomit—calling it art, as if seat belts held you closer,
driving towards a vanishing ecosystem, highway—dark

cd list #6 what haunting were your eyes exit

low theory sonnet

there's blood on the keys
dirt precipitation in my left
iris / a chilling renunciation
low-theory headache / wishing
      i was bed rotting with you too
with the sunrise of my camouflage
mirror staring back at me, grinning

      i stab my eyes to meet phosphenes
not just today but yesterday too
      i tell you that when i feel the flow
of energy which is not visible
like the whisper of a kiss or monday
morning stillness there is always
perhaps more humanity within [the] outside of
                a cage—

one day i realized i was a cell
on an excel sheet,   [the]
taste of digital steel still lingers

are we like somewhere in sacramento

today i saw a chrysalis & thought of you
waiting for my algorithm to digitize my
own nostalgia, way i feel invisible in july
christmas—there is a tree inside a room
somewhere in los angeles—have you seen
them, behind the curtain of the firework
sky lawn, behind the tongue-tied solo cup
martini impression—sucks being the cool-
est kid in the room but when i entered the
fred meyer for my taxes & a lobotomy
there was something about denial that i
refused to chew, yet everyone watched me
lacing up my surveilled body inside fiber-
glass container, guilty of everything

rainy day triple sonnet crown

after Dorothy Chan

i'm somewhere stuck between gloom
& an afterlife i didn't get to choose
ash in my pocket, way glitter never
leaves earth, way microplastics tongue
our lungs, way poems smear karmic
countenances while you drive home
resurgence is not in fact in the eye
of the bed-holder but cupped
within your blue cherry nova supreme
yucca—how coming in the morning
changes perspective on the realm
of enlightenment, only borderline
respectfully, as i hear the city tremble
in the apple pie gut of my gray california

someone in the neighborhood is more
miserable at the day, won't appreciate
shadow-play with venetian blinds
won't ever hear the whisper of my pink
trumpet like when celestial beings read
me byron in the leviathan of my mind
they said my voice was marigold—way
you think of it when you think of me
don't lie, semblance of sound is only
fleeting because it miscommunicates
with your body, perhaps the ghosts in
my childhood home's vault only want
to remember their recurring dream
where they stare intensely at kitchen tile

dusky blue, way a song is only sad when you
remember it, way i see you seeing me—
there are moments of light hidden behind
digression, this being one of those moments—
sometimes, i remember reading about my death
waiting around in velveteen-style to stumble on
a poem to save me—way it wasn't this one or
that one but you—hidden underneath this son-
net; something about portals & the transient
whisper of liminality inside spaces where rain
cannot exist but instead is merely hypothesis
outside, i'm somewhere between streetlight
& shadow in the pocket of green neon age—
what do you call a city that rains in endless sun

nostalgia for samsara

1. a list poem for gaza—
2. art ought to mirror back the flesh materiality it reflects, whereas to spark direct action in the city is something more than poetry but if theory is thy celestial body, then perchance the very action of the word is verb—is poem, is home without borderland
3. on the third day of spring, april, thinking how i'd reach to find you again, every 1000 years over, only to embrace & share breath with you, break bread, make-out, cry aloud, buy avocados in the overpriced-gentrified supermarket
4. i've begun the habit again, collecting blue stuff
5. i see a familiar angel, on my way to work, one with silver in the smile, weaving in & out of pockets of smog, motor oil, buzzing exhaust, no bread during pandemic, no free parking in an election year
6. let this radicalize you
7. whereas you can imagine such energy or perhaps there is such a place, in response to my second strophe in this apology
8. nauseated inside the algorithmically numbing scroll of instantly streamed genocide, my ancestor from el valle reassures me of such a thing called a reckoning
9. today, i wanna rot in bed all day with you, buy a new camera lens, take a photo of all the outside blue
10. in this apology when i mention the term "apology," i humbly mean it in the aristotelian sense, *metadata is often the most reptilian mistress* mumbles the ai bot lodged inside my william carlos williams
11. *these are not mountains*, i scribble on a polaroid, instant karma wrapped in cellophane, palms nest for owls disguised as brujas, past the skate park pocket check blacktop—past my nostalgia for samsara
12. *this is just to say*, in the aspen of my dizziness i witness a bushel of yellow flowers, somewhere in oregon
13. in *broken conversation*, my brother whispers the bad news, one winter knowing there's something frightening about tranquil days, blue lavender asphalt cempasúchtil ash
14. insert here a humanist non sequitur, a call for your very own forbearance, a grief that is not only heavy but fluid, that which is languid—remember that i too was but a glimmer in the transient dots & dashes of your void

SOMETIMES, I WISH I COULD
FAX THIS TO YOU

wave of mutilation

night i *cease[d] to resist* / i forgot to *give my goodbye[s]*—
choke-swallowed bath water till i taste porcelain sky

my father found me / a forgotten poem / wet cold drenched
my left cerebral hemisphere—blue quivery shy

underwater / under influenced—there's too much pain
in living / there's too much living in pain—instead / i lie

water in lungs / i couldn't feel temperature of a room
on fire / hey / what was the last song you heard before i died

before filling the tub & staining it with marine tears
before searching for me at the bottom of blue goodbyes

before you find me in before / i *drive my car into*
the ocean / you call my name in three letters—say goodbye

face ghost

remember when you said / *there is weight in the words we've said*
speeding down the 101 north / bypass traffic / i quietly said

begrudgingly / where do you drive when i sleep-hide away
from you / streetlights mirror / windshield glare amber yellow red

burning my nausea / your shadow listless tact / your fave shade
as if betrayal in sleep didn't mean much happening from bed

before you confessed / painted your hubris pigeon gray or
red / you deep shouted & wished your washed concrete conscious dead

sometimes your haunting reappears in sidewalk undertones
shadow southbound slack jawed side slumped sleepy eyed—who said

anything about tunnel dusk forgiveness—yet you yeet—
jimmied quiet again / *same ghosts that keep me awake* are dead

sister ray

passenger seat white miata coupe whiplash / *searching for my*
mainline / somewhere near east los or red jagged careen of thy

pounding skull / as if turning up the volume / distorted
slack brings us closer / zero traffic relief / getting high

& driving like sharing eucharist / communal & less
heavy / why were we driving fast / car seat confessions shy

vomited / green beers & vicodin / no cup holder to
hold my backwashed neurosis / maybe if we crash & die

on the 710 / we might cure our blue messy headache resonance
sharing cigarettes inside brake light staccato sighs

before i crack split my head open like yolk you say / *hey*
jim / *don't you know* / *you'll stain the carpet* unless you twice die

moon river

if i clench my jaw tight enough / i can still taste sour slur
broken promises / *oh* / *dream maker* / muddy wet tears puddled

dashboard molasses / i was your mary magdalene sigh
blue loud quiet whisper / clandestine ache in your throat knuckled

city streetlights fractured glare on your black frames / ruptured
soliloquies—sorrys / illiterate refrains doubled

in double-parked penumbra transgressions / remember / drunk
crying to moon river / your shaky fog voice amber bubbled

i can still taste it if i lick my own hippocampus
your honey brown eyes blood orange red / you slurred messy muddled

my name / called to me in three letters / i'm sorry i hurt
you then / you said / *jim* / *you heartbreaker* / then you quickly chuckled

CEMPASÚCHTIL ASH

el otro lado de la noche es una noche sin noche, sin tierra,
sin casas, sin cuartos, sin muebles, sin gente

—Jaime Sáenz

i said too much didn't i didn't i

on my way out
      the door i try leaving my metallic

manic depression to get into my
      steel cage—how many times can
i say car in a poem without men-

tioning the road   peel out
      left jab on atlantic to daydream
on the 710 to the 5   how many

poems can i write about roads
      before i become roadkill, a skid
mark on concrete   in my anguish

      i quiz myself on the difference
between chronos time & kairos time
cause i'm always late & no one

is caressing this anxiety or fingering
      the postulate of my confessions—

here's this secret—
      i'll whisper it telepathically

do you feel it   (?)

i can almost taste the snare of my own language ///

*

my very own ego
        death smiling back

                even hamlet gripped his sheets tightly
                once to try & make himself disappear

                a ghost fragmented memory coffined in
                periphery ceremonial mask, if you show
                me your parasitic apathy, i'll show you
                      the zirconium ash in my brain

*

past sidewalk concrete porno silver traffic, past forgotten
temporal lobe recollections, past elegiac passenger seat
confessions, past hypnosis highway cruise control cybersex

        this is what folx call lockjaw or bone-tired depression
           you can spoil it your damn self if you lick
              the blue cherry ambulance cry of my suffering

*

i kissed my own transorbital lobotomy
night i traded it for twilight sleep

                          inside the drunk tank pink centerfolds
                          of my swinishness renunciation

                          even i moist the categorical imperative
                          before hiding

                              *

i keep drowning in my own fragments

i keep stroking my neurasthenia—
          even in slate-trashed-streets
          i chant the four noble truths

i keep chasing lights in tunnels
          it doesn't rain in los angeles
          my puddled mind wet neon blue

still lodged in the lavender of my throat, the city,

              come   find it

no fun/no love

bludgeon the cop in your head—
      mouse trap to the dome

your dead won't hold you

deus ex machina come, crash
                      into me

this isn't an axiom

cerebral car crash on silver streets

----

someone asks if i really like the dodgers

while you breastfeed the one that survived

it always comes back to foucault
& the proliferation of surveillance
you watching me watching you
    watching my own death on t.v.

so what if i'm no fun anymore…

define praxis or agape or gargantuan

define my long list of confessions
        my brief prayers / my sacrilege sacrifice

----

yes   maybe your absence is a presence
                       maybe my sleep deprived molcajete eyes
are rummaging for *honest sleep*

                       can't find a decent parking space on
the east or the west side
                       can't find the little halo tucked
        away in my conglomerate lethargy

----

on south pasadena ave, palms glittering
santa anas blanket my private vigil

in a city of parking lot infrastructures
it isn't enough to try & find you >>>

yes   this is an apology

                    but in the aristotelian
sense—flat cherry coke bad day hood lyric

          —a new american classic

whisper it ///

on gray salt paloma 108th street, owls at dusk
are pantoums perched on palms—they too, forgive

abecedarian 21

after opening all the letters
before dawn did you bathe by
city streetlights? did you crash
during daybreak driving towards death?
even the 405 reminds me of you—
frantically fighting fatigue again in
gridlock, are you still afraid of glaucoma
hurting your eyes? has it hurt? have you eaten?
irrevocably. letters from the department of
justice—jaundiced & jammed in pillowcases
knapsacked quilted—keeping em' safe to
listen for the voice of your father. landmarking
most of his memories or motor functions.
not knowing if ice will show up
or when you'll finally lose your osteoporotic keys,
parked patiently somewhere near abandonment &
quietude. quivering in prayer for quintessence.
remembering your father's ruddy laugh because
someday they might shadow lock him in silver steel.
tomorrow never really smells like tuesday,
untying the knot in your throat as you hop in—
veer towards the left lane, missing the exit.
windshield glass reflected windows of your iris
xeroxed by glare. 'xactly what freeway are you in?
you never tell me. you just drive off towards
zirconium streets zigzagging through traffic.
                              are you still there?

july in rain

sidewalk drunk with wine
water & you tell me *chance*
is never random. daydreaming
inside fossil fuel extinction, waylaid
on the corner of dorothy ave
itching for fog fluorescent melodies—

city street silence enveloped her silver tongue
around my neocortex like velvet eyes
                              kissing sapphire

in the afterglow of bruises & symbiotic
whispers, city eyes charcoal rainwater
sleepy like a david berman bridge—

i only wanna die in your eyes, as city
              waits for me on amethyst streets

phosphorescent   calmness trickling
              down wet hyacinths praying for stone like july in rain

marigold & fugue in d minor

x presses keys
as blood stains desert
floors in sonora & sueños
americano are devoured
by vultures or lack of water.
el desierto es muy misterioso
they tell me as white crosses
are tucked inside tierra
in southern arizona, rosary
beads glisten tucked
in dirt or else clenched
like yellowed cavities—x
says they miss me
as children are crammed
in cages without their mother's
heartbeat en la frontera, sighing
as they mismatch their socks
or else the sign of the cross
& the women in el camino del diablo
rem sleep of caquis & rain
as they shove their palms
into sky like digging
out clouds—they dream
of stone while they fist
their sleep lids, whispering
to guadalupe—& x
is still trying to play bach
as children huddle sleepless
in adelanto or bedford, texas
weep like pregnant saguaros
while bones bleached & abandoned

glitter like snow in desert. x
hammers the piano—pounding
percussive instrument while a mother
muffles chamomile prayers in fluorescent
light & ruby saguaro silence
of the jaundiced sonora desert
sleepless—3:29 a.m. & i ask,
do you think dirt disapproves
                              of anything?

realized i wasn't enough

morning i tasted exhaust
       fumes & savored pink sunset
       soliloquies—you didn't call
because you've been busy
       swimming inside someone
          else's ocean iris

my voice   blanketed dust
taste of blood   or magnesium

before i become a preemptive
       washrag—i'd swallow pavement
to confess pigeon city street
       sidewalk algorithms—maybe
the metadata lodged inside
my frontal lobe makes me less
lonely; wet streets pornographic

you told me about your forgetful
epiphanic morning but only through
       clairvoyance & only after forgetting
the last two letters of my name—
       some abstract riddle about mortality
& coming to terms with being made
up of chemicals—i shrugged & laughed

how many sighs like tongued pavement
       when you woke tangled in wires again

realized i wasn't enough
        night i caressed my splintered headache—
shrugged you off
like the ugliness of your laugh
                fading into a dark room

we lose our fleshy bodies, our corporeality

[don't we?]

look, maybe *i should've crashed the car the night i drove* back home—95 on the 105 trafficless weeknight—i turned off my headlights just to taste invincibility like invisibility yawning reckless casting sigils during every other exit or else telepathically swallowing these shrouded fragments

swallow fluoride electric city blue trudging pavement as if i were the only one suffering upon suffering forgetting my keys at the edge of neurosis daydreaming cacti prickly & sheen...

[cascading]

parked
                  no head
          lights sleepy bad breath mourning last night's
                  ash caught yellowed teeth barefoot dizzy tip
                              toeing on laminated brown-red

i finally woke, bit lip twice, the third time
—eyes rolled to the back of my rolodex
half ass wish lids half closed:
shadow staining simultaneously surrendering my somatic samsara

grease up the grooves
          shapeshifting with the algorithm forget to take my meds

cause they remind me of god inside television—
snakeskin boots near the cavity of my therapist phone calls hot-shit
confessions

                              i burned humming scent fingertips ember
                              with attitude or else caressed my zirconium
                          amygdala till i was a little less lonely cause
                              maybe masturbating my pain is praxis

[maybe]

the bark
                    in my voice   is sunrise   in pavement eye

look, just forget it—so what if i don't remember the last song i listened to
before crashing the car
            before glass shattering clavicle
                    before bruise jaw kissing leather
                              windshield wipers without rain

i vomited morning till daybreak turned pink forgetting recipe to my favorite
hematoma in pitch
                anyway—

you lost all your l.a. privileges

—i'd neo-radiate
your old address on the pretty tips of my skull

wandering again—cloudy-crashing
                              cyber spaces—trying to exit the playlists etched
                                        in your peripherals—

& i hate writing poems about [you]—i overhear on the green line
          searching for the gold thread of my unlucky tooth

look, the pigeon tells the rat, remember:

salt of my coastal line / vomit enough until i no longer sense your touch / your
mouth swallowed waves / you still read text that isn't blue lit / my back keeps
getting jammed / the wine stains on my desk are getting messy / you still fumble
around for your keys in the morning / last night i rearranged my astrology chart
/ i couldn't read my fucking tea leaves even if i cried / you still eat razor wire to
taste sunshine / frustrations rose in undertone / city lilac convergence on the daisy
of my eye / unfurled oceanic breeze / polar ice caps melting your crooked smile /
anxieties abandoned on pch / what other line should i unsubscribe /

                    & i hate writing poems about global warming but here i am again

& you roll your eyes sliding off the bed
          french press depression—

          four-minute timer dripping away groggy sighs . . .

—& maybe you are tone-deaf—*i ain't mad at ya'*

—my voice only lingers in waves

micro
        cosmic—different color of your iris

i stain my mind merlot to fantasize about my
        sleep phantoms

tonguing your fluorescent crown past my nostalgic grave, whisked breath
walking up the second
        story of my low theory headache, as i too, shuttered at my own vertebrae

i've been dreaming in exile

        my triptych dusty
        unsettled or unenthused /

        —three hail marys for you & modernity

you ever wish you were everywhere inside / in june you were your own bruise /
in kitchen morning / what were your last words

you(r) call

you call & tell me about your new life in koreatown
        you mention x—not owning a drafting table
you tell me you finally spoke to your dad—
        the face he made when you told him you'd be leaving
the face you remember him making when you told him
                we'd lost…

        you call & tell me about not visiting mammoth & only
            getting one parking space at your new place but you forget
to tell me about your nausea & vomiting about how tired
        the meds make you feel—chalk coloring your mouth—
i ask if they make you drowsy but i know—what i really
        wanna know is if you think of me when you close your eyes
           & bite your tongue

you call & tell me you miss me as if betrayal
        wasn't a four-letter word as if best friends cupped palms
drinking hemlock you rest all of your clothes on my side
        of the bed—you tell me the weight seems familiar—seems
like someone sleeping next to you without having
           to invite anyone

        you call & ask if i've heard the new bright eyes album
        you laugh a little because you know the answer
you call our ottoman a stool & swear it'll really bring your new place
        together—you tell me you're really finding yourself in places
i've vanished—*i've been trying to cut all my dead hair off*—
        you tell me   calling from x's   her home smells
like tortillas & cardamom but i still haven't asked what color her room is
          —you like secrets

you call your voice home—you think it's kitsch
              to keep contact—i keep writing letters you'll never
read scribbled cipher in tangerine   i forget to burn
              them   you're not surprised—the only time you think
                            of me is when you pray—

              you call & tell me you never pray—you confess
                            in one-liners you tell me you still wear dresses smeared
              with subtle forgotten scents   sometimes   you even shade
                            your eyes red before they run smudgy after your catnaps
              on the leather sofa
                            —you keep telling me—

your call wakes me knee deep inside my ruminations'
              ruminations—sometimes hearing your lisp like most times
still stings yesterday's penumbra of my blue voice—

              you call & ask me if i remember washing your feet
                            night you were dancing barefoot & champagne
              your pale skin colored pavement sticky
                            with that night's shuffled playlist—
              you cried handing me soap sitting at the edge
                            of bathtub-porcelain-stained-lavender

your call paints me nostalgic
              hands clasped trudging little tokyo pavement
smell of warm-broth-stale-urine green eyed & wandering

                            you call & ask if i still write poems about you

your call caresses my aphasia—

      your voice diffracted swims inside my cornea
         you still laugh like you're the only one in a room

                      you tell me you lit candles for y
            who never got to see your green eyes turn red

     you call & tell me she keeps appearing in places
          she's not—a glimmer whisper kissing your amygdala

in infinite resignation there is peace & repose

this is the way the world ends
this is the way the world ends
this is the way [my] *world ends*
        not with a bang, but with a [splat]
a shot to the dome / car crash inside my neocortex

i'm giving you this pain now
        murder mundane memory

this is no [closure]
this is ritual
        blood sacrifice or else sanctification

show me the sanskrit word for vedic

this is an offering
an ofrenda inside my [hollow] eye

freeway ghost

cause i rather be ghost
rummaging l.a. city dizzy lost
& fractal, remember, tangled
the car again in cul-de-sac candelabra

crashed my blue voice box on cesar chavez
bridge & laughed at myself, swallowing
sunset skies on sixth street

   —this is not a poem, this is an exorcism

     cause i rather be ghost yawning sleep eyes
     heavy driving the 101, scribbled songs
     in polycarbonate, call it a mixtape, abandon it in asphalt,
     i'll find you there—i'll be the lamb wrapped in cellophane
     hidden under parataxis icebox / cause i rather be ghost like
     lodged underneath fingernails / said i'd swallow six
     streets to replace my own fragmented voice /

this is not a poem

     this is a reckoning / can you taste this—tectonic novelty

nights i drove in impermanence, headlights in pitch—710 or else the 105,
driving the 91 eastbound, something sad playing on car stereo, shadow-play
on the highway, pedal pushing 95 past the overpass, radiator howling, cast shadow
glistening in freeway light, blurry syncopated images of cars & walls & signs &
palmettos, coming to me all a posteriori

—i swear the city hides in the back of my lungs,
even now

poem for yourself

after Graham Foust

you freeway worship inside melancholic ofrenda of traffic similes tonguing the depression palm fronds of your lily iris

why do you keep driving? / where are you driving into?

sometimes when you wake / maybe you ain't fun any longer…you ain't any longer fun

you realize karma only seems a gag gift when you're gagging on your own suffering upon suffering

some will say you've used this line before—so what / this is the coda before the timpani roll

you ever miss the morning light in the dining room when you sat with yourself & premature grief / cascading yolk sun piercing pearl venetian blinds

now all you have is your jacaranda listlessness / the attempts of drowning in a bathtub / your father dug you out of porcelain—evening spelunking

who will cure the sleepy hamlet within your renunciation

this ain't a poem about a dead city or a dead poet / you ever wax wane on the 710 or the 5 / yellow tobacco stains your acidic amnesia

you ever hold yourself it's insurmountable

in that dream you never had yesterday / a familiar face appeared but said nothing

in mourning / you gesticulate your own apathy shaking grief from your marrow

this poem won't hold you / won't be a mirror but a wall of opaque glass that cries for shattering

you suffocate your memories on slate los angeles streets / smog sweat & gum /
obfuscating the impermanence of a city built on top of cheap infrastructure

nothing permanent in l.a.

sometimes when you wake / you ain't funny any longer...

city boiler heat gasoline exhaust / skid row piss cigarette / freeway carcass splat
ash / los angeles in graveyard motion

close your palms near street preachers / won't sell your dna to be less lonely / it
never rains in l.a. / sidewalk wet & neurotic

ocular headache loverot surveillance / wilshire & vermont concrete moaning
/ still waiting for godot on the green line / reading your elegy on whittier
boulevard / scavenging your burial

strung out in los angeles / graffiti scrawl on green metal freeway signs / barbed
wire counterfeit 4th street dissent / cardboard house dreams / encampment
carbon pressure & road gravel / south los angeles street / chokehold cataracts
burnt rubber / angels drowsy in gutters

will you hold them

you're on the 5 in 5 / $5.55 for a gallon / you keep driving till you car crash
the subie / you keep driving to miss exits / you keep driving to cast sigils
on the overpass / you keep driving to make wishes every time a streetlight
switches / you keep driving through bridges / you keep driving to make a
purple flower reappear on the dash—call it lavender asphalt...

call it a vanishing act . . .

sing a lilac wish / wrap it in plastic / send it to someone you love / either through telepathy or landline; cut here

----

your catholic worry grins at your guilty of everything anguish

riot inside your head

careening into the k-rail exiting the 710 north / airbags kissing your face / red-glare paramedic lights erotic

—have i lost you

really—have i lost you

your obsessive-compulsive disorder often the loudest voice in the room / three clicks & you're just as lucky as dorothy with red slippers for sighs

you know—no one is really thinking of you—you know

tear drops in bar bathrooms & parking lots or on the passenger side of paved roads / / a celestial promise to the void / a glinting pluralistic prayer

continuously motion sick searching for ephemerality

you don't eat

continuously running on e

[your] body is a witch & [you are] burning it

your car both grave & urn

you keep stroking your despair to engorge your own depression

even your lágrimas are sacrilege / it doesn't rain in los angeles

abrahamic anguish riddled in non-bad faith hearts misery / bloodletting is choice not doctrine in sacrificial tradition

no sympathy for false dichotomies / you can't not not choose / syncretic apology

what freeway exit to heaven for the existentialist who marries the opening dilemma to the myth of sisyphus / the only question worth long thought

i nearly lost you

wake / smell hood concrete / pavement won't hold you—even if you are kissing ground

catatonic in early dark afternoon glow / los angeles is ghost / your breath—shy soliloquy / kind you hang on the fridge or sing out loud when you're zero traffic on the 710

i promise you everything

you ain't meditating in traffic / you're shedding metadata in your steel carbon cage

& you keep second guessing yourself / so much that 12:12 appears as both annotation & prayer

& you keep chasing ghosts in crescendo afterglow / searching for your abuelito in the ocean corneas of your grandmother's eyes / graphite & ocean & the kind of beautiful that is lonesome sometimes / you need to stop yourself from asking where your papá pancho is / cause he ain't in his favorite chair / cause he ain't on his side of the couch / cause he ain't wringing his hands—yelling at the dodgers / cause he ain't feeding his pajaritos / cause he ain't tasting bitter drops of dark coffee / cause he ain't playing baraja / cause he ain't suffering upon suffering any longer

he is in the thirst of your grandmother's voice / 24 years of dialysis / so you pollute your lungs to get closer to the pain

are you the persona non grata of the poem? is this where it ends to begin

you cross yourself on bullis & long beach / on paloma streets painted steel blue / you hear los angeles ache / while lowriders hum in sleepy street soliloquies / it never rains in l.a.

you keep fisting your sleep lids in search for your neon prayer garland / you figure an amber chrysalis holds god's syllabic tercet

now that your mamá licha is hummingbird you speak softly & listen

does anyone else pray for you

you keep interrupting your beginner's mind / callejero heat chamber swollen on top the precipice of heartache & loss like a cinema classic

someone somewhere is probably thinking of you

la virgencita esta contigo

you keep saying you wanna build an altar / you keep saying you'll pray a little more than you confess but it all stays in your clouded mind & there's rain continuously on a loop puddling your brain—just smell the cempasúchtil / ain't like you don't wanna anyway...

how many ways can i say it doesn't rain in l.a.

never have i ever...

wiped your tears on the 4th street bridge / hazy streetlight glittering the
angel asleep on blue graphite pavement; city doesn't whisper / it car crashes
whimper—it roars

listen

NOTES

"We died prodigiously..." p. 3 The epigraph is from Jack Spicer, "Berkeley in Time of Plague," *My Vocabulary Did This to Me: The Collected Poetry of Jack Spicer.*

"another freeway poem—an ars poetica written near the 710" p. 7 The poem is written in response to a comment I only write about freeways and roads. This ars poetica addresses the recurring question of why we write. The recurring line throughout the book "i can't breathe" was the repeated plea of George Floyd, a Black man who was restrained and later murdered by a white police officer. The line "eat her cancer..." is a remix nod from Nirvana, "Heart-Shaped Box," the album *In Utero.*

"voicemail i ching" p. 21 The phrase "tell me about god..." is from an old sermon former professor Dr. Bruce Hanson would mention in lectures. The phrase "fade into you" is from Mazzy Star's song of same name. This poem was first performed as part of the group exhibition *Spell/ing*, REEF Los Angeles, curated by Irene Gil-Ramon and Julia Sáenz Lorduy.

"poem about my uncle" p. 27 After Jose Hernandez Diaz, a surrealist approach to the prose poem, which this once was. The phrase "there are moments we call..." is a remix nod to La Dispute, "Hudsonville, MI 1956," the album *Rooms of the House.*

"room 237" p. 28 The lines "all work & no / play..." and "darling, light of my life" are from Stanley Kubrick's film, *The Shining.*

"listening to your playlist while driving made me feel like i was in your car again going around l.a." p. 30 Lines from a text message by Damian Wang in response to a W.S. Merwin poem read in class with Harryette Mullen. The lines "for no reason at all" from ROAR's EP title track "I Can't Handle Change." The phrase "it's the saddest ones..." is a remix nod to Bright Eyes, "Laura Laurent," the album *LIFTED or The Story Is in the Soil, Keep Your Ear to the Ground.* The line "are some of the old colors still there" is from Merwin's poem "No Believer," *Garden Time.*

"song of bleeding throats" p. 34 Title is a remix of Walt Whitman's "Song of the bleeding throat," part 4 of "When Lilacs Last in the Dooryard Bloom'd," in later revisions of *Leaves of Grass*. The lines "in sleeper holds" and "we're choking…" are from L.A. hardcore band Dangers, "Loose Cigarettes," in the album *The Bend in the Break*, written by vocalist Alfred Brown IV. The allusion of Eric Garner is present in the song, a Black man who was murdered by cops for selling loose cigarettes. The recurring line throughout the book "i can't breathe" reappears here—these were the pleas of Eric Garner.

"five-car collision playlist: a sonnet about freeways" p. 39 The line "i cry not for myself" is from the song "I Hear A Symphony," by The Supremes.

"rainy day triple sonnet crown" p. 43 The poem owes to Dorothy Chan's myriad ways of elevating and experimenting with sonnets, especially as related to the triple sonnet crown. See also Bernadette Mayer.

"nostalgia for samsara" p. 45 The phrase "collecting blue stuff" is a remix nod to Maggie Nelson, *Bluets*. The phrase "this is just to say" is from William Carlos Williams' poem of the same name. The phrase "broken conversation" is from Charlotte Brontë, *Jane Eyre*.

"wave of mutilation" p. 49 The lines "cease[d] to resist…" and "drive my car into…" are from the Pixies, "Wave of Mutilation," the album *Doolittle*.

"face ghost" p. 50 The phrases "there is weight in the words…" and "same ghosts…" are from Touché Amoré, "Face Ghost," the album *Parting the Sea Between Brightness and Me*.

"sister ray" p. 51 The phrases "searching for my mainline" and "don't you know…" are from The Velvet Underground, "Sister Ray," the album *White Light/White Heat*.

"moon river" p. 52 Phrases "oh dream maker" and "you heartbreaker" from the song "Moon River" sung by Audrey Hepburn, lyrics by Johnny Mercer, in the film *Breakfast at Tiffany's*.

"el otro lado de la noche…" p. 53 Epigraph from the epic poem by Jaime Sáenz, "La Noche," *La Noche*.

"no fun/no love" p. 58 The phrase "honest sleep" is from Touché Amoré, the album *…To the Beat of a Dead Horse*.

"july in rain" p. 62 The line "i only wanna die in your eyes" is from Silver Jews "How to Rent a Room," the album *The Natural Bridge*.

"marigold & fugue in d minor" p. 63 The lines "do you think…" are from Dean Young, "The Death of André Breton," *Shock by Shock*.

"we lose our fleshy bodies, our corporeality" p. 67 The title is from Philip K. Dick, *The Three Stigmata of Palmer Eldritch*, spoken by the character Fran discussing the hallucinogenic drug Can-D. The lines "i should have crashed…" are from Citizen, "The Night I Drove Alone," the album *Youth*.

"you lost all your l.a. privileges" p. 69 The title borrows from Quentin Tarantino, the film *Pulp Fiction*, spoken by the character Marsellus Wallace. The phrase "i ain't mad at ya'" is a remix nod to Tupac Shakur's track of a similar name.

"in infinite resignation there is peace & repose" p. 74 The title borrows from Søren Kierkegaard, the philosophical work *Fear and Trembling*. The phrase "this is the way the world ends…" is from the poem by T.S. Eliot, "The Hollow Men." The phrase "murder memory" is from hardcore band Title Fight, "Murder Your Memory," the album *Hyperview*.

"poem for yourself" p. 76 After Graham Foust, with inspiration after reading his poem "To Graham Foust on the Morning of His Fortieth Birthday," *To Anacreon in Heaven and Other Poems*. This poem was written from a prompt given by Anthony McCann in a CalArts poetry workshop that asked for the writing of a self-addressed poem, which I'd never done. I ask, "how do you tell yourself something, are you able to hold the mirror up close to yourself—is this practice in decathexis or else vulnerability?" The refrain "suffering upon suffering" throughout the book is from the Buddhist teaching of the Four Noble Truths. The phrase "strung out in los angeles" a remix nod to Døves and Wicca Phase Springs Eternal, "Better," the mixtape / dj-set *ULTRACLUB4K*. The phrase "you're on the 5 in 5" is a remix nod to Touché Amoré "Palm Dreams," the album *Stage Four*. The line "[your] body is a witch…" is from the poem by Eavan Boland, "Anorexic," *In Her Own Image*. The line "the opening dilemma to the myth of sisyphus" references the beginning statement in the philosophical essay of the same name by Albert Camus. The phrase "i nearly lost you" is from Empire! Empire! (I Was a Lonely Estate), "Ribbon," the album *You Will Eventually Be Forgotten*. The line "reading your own elegy on whittier boulevard" refers to a historic street in East Los Angeles, better known as the street, where the Chicano Moratorium held a peaceful, youth-led anti-Vietnam War demonstration in 1970 which ultimately degenerated into police brutality. It also was the backdrop of the classic 1974 Chicano performance by ASCO, *First Supper (After a Major Riot)* shot by Harry Gamboa Jr., featuring Patssi Valdez, Humberto Sandoval, Willie Herrón, and Gronk—depicting in this brief absurd moment the epicenter of East L.A. Chicano culture and its history of overcoming injustice.

ACKNOWLEDGMENTS

Grateful acknowledgment and big love to the following publications in which these poems first appeared, sometimes in earlier versions:

Altadena Poetry Review: Anthology: "persimmons"

Broken Lens Journal: "song of bleeding throats," "no fun/no love," "are we like somewhere in sacramento"

Diode Poetry Journal: "abecedarian 21," "rainy day triple sonnet crown"

Dunce Codex Magazine: "you lost all your l.a. privileges"

Furious Pure Magazine: "are we like somewhere in sacramento," "i am no longer a list of attachments," "i wanna be unsubscribed from my digital vertigo of transient escalator rendezvous" ["new romantic or can't you smell the world burning"]

Maintenant: A Journal of Contemporary DADA Writing & Art, Three Rooms Press: "poem about my uncle" ["prose poem about my uncle"]

Poetry Goes to the Movies: An Anthology, Pacific Coast Poetry Series: "room 237"

The Los Angeles Press: "persimmons"

The Sparring Artists: Literary Anthology of Sparring With Beatnik Ghosts, Mystic Boxing Commission: "voicemail i ching"

Westwind: UCLA's Journal of the Arts: "collapsed lung," "marigold & fugue in d minor," "listening to your playlist while driving made me feel like i was in your car again going around l.a.," "you(r) call"

For my parents Maggie and Jaime, with my love. Thank you for all your support and encouragement—this book is for you, always. Thank you for taking me to all the shows, the games, the plays, all the readings, and for always encouraging me to create art. For my brothers Omar, Angel, and Ivan, thank you for being my light all these years, I've survived because of you, this book is for you. For my sister Gaby, always my confidant.

For my grandparents, mi Papá Buelo, mi Mamá Licha, mi Papá Pancho, y mi Mamá Nene.

For my familia Vega, both in L.A. and Michoacán, I think of you often, los quiero!

For my familia Magaña, thank you for shaping me and raising me, this is for you.

For my familia Quintero, especially Benji and Teresa for taking me in.

Tremendous gratitude to Gail Wronsky and Chuck Rosenthal and the entire What Books Press team for believing in this book, your trust and encouragement mean the world.

To my mentors and teachers: Ms. Sanchez, Mrs. Padilla, Mrs. Budak, Maggie Nelson, Janice Lee, Janna Anderson, Bruce Hanson, Brandon Floerke, Richard Levesque, Annie Liu, Michael Mangan, Fred D'Aguiar, Harryette Mullen, Brian Kim Stefans, Colleen Jaurretche, Tisa Bryant, Gabrielle Civil, Matias Viegener, Andrea Fontenot, Wanda Coleman, Sesshu Foster, Diana Khoi Nguyen, Roberto Tejada, Michael Leong, Prageeta Sharma, Douglas Kearney, Anthony McCann, and not least of all to my editor and longtime mentor Karen Kevorkian for all of your trust in my work and encouragement—your mentorship and guidance is a treasured line I keep coming back to.

To my past collaborators, co-conspirators, and friends: Damian Wang, Alice Fulmer, Kenneth Reveiz, Ica Sadagat, Julia Sáenz Lorduy, Nikki Ochoa, Joseph Laury, Josh Wolpert, Rosa Evangelina Beltrán, Alexey Greggs, z.No scott, Patrick Hogan, Anthony Garcia, and all other past peers in workshops, in and out of classrooms who helped me find my voice and nurtured me with your friendship.

To Beyond Baroque and the current crew—Quentin Ring, Iván Salinas, Genesis Perez, Rhiannon Cielos Chavez, Nicholas Forman, Jody Zellen, Francesca Corrado, Megan Leahy, & Eric Ahlberg for your help in cultivating a poetry community in our little space in Venice and for your encouragement of my work.

Thanks to Gronk for the gift of art and friendship, to ash good for your design and friendship—to Harry Gamboa Jr. for the photo and friendship.

Gratitude to the communities of Lynwood and Los Angeles, who have in many instances and in many ways made these cities home, and for all the open doors that have led me to continue the work we yet still need to do.

For Olive for being my sunshine every single morning.

For Gladys—thank you for all the love, art, devotion, faith, lessons, experiences, and trust you give me each day. Don't you forget it for one second, it's all for you.

JIMMY VEGA is the child of Mexican immigrants, a Chicano Los Angeles poet, educator, and interdisciplinary artist. He holds a BA from UCLA in English and an MFA from the California Institute of the Arts, Creative Writing program. vega has presented work at REDCAT, Poetic Research Bureau, The Sims Library of Poetry, Associated Writing Programs (Seattle, 2023) conference, Beyond Baroque, the Mark Taper Auditorium at the Los Angeles Central Library, the Thinking Its Presence conference, and at REEF Los Angeles as part of the group exhibition *Spelling*. vega is commissioned to write new work by the city of Los Angeles, is a former English Language Learning Faculty Fellow at CalArts, and presently is the Associate Director of Beyond Baroque Literary / Arts Center. He lives in Los Angeles on unceded Tongva Land. *zirconium ash* is vega's debut poetry collection. JIMMY-VEGA.COM

WHAT BOOKS PRESS

AN IMPRINT OF

THE GLASS TABLE

C O L L E C T I V E

LOS ANGELES

All WHAT BOOKS feature cover art by Los Angeles painter, printmaker, muralist, and theater and performance artist GRONK. A founding member of ASCO, Gronk collaborates with the LA and Santa Fe Operas and the Kronos Quartet. His work is found in the Corcoran, Smithsonian, LACMA, and Riverside Art Museum's Cheech Marin collection.

As a small, independent press, we urge our readers to support independent publishers and booksellers. This is easily done by visiting our website, WhatBooksPress.com, where you can purchase books directly from us or from Bookshop.org

2025

Inside the Umber Iris
ERIK MANUEL SOTO
WINNER OF THE GRONK
NICANDRO FIRST BOOK PRIZE
POEMS

Persistence of Singing Woods
JOHN COLBURN
STORIES

River of Angels
STEPHEN COOPER
STORIES

Jukebox
PATTY SEYBURN
POEMS

zirconium ash
JIMMY VEGA
POEMS

2024

The Manuscripts
KEVIN ALLARDICE
NOVEL

Father Elegies
STELLA HAYES
POEMS

Slow Return
PAUL LIEBER
POEMS

Dreamer Paradise
DAVID QUIROZ
POEMS

How to Capture Carbon
CAMERON WALKER
STORIES

2023

God in Her Ruffled Dress
LISA B (LISA BERNSTEIN)
POEMS

Figures of Wood
MARÍA PÉREZ-TALAVERA
TRANSLATED BY PAUL FILEV
NOVEL

A Plea for Secular Gods: Elegies
BRYAN D. PRICE
POEMS

Nightfall Marginalia
SARAH MACLAY
POEMS

Romance World
TAMAR PERLA CANTWELL
STORIES

2022

No One Dies in Palmyra Ohio
HENRY ELIZABETH CHRISTOPHER
NOVEL

Us Clumsy Gods
ASH GOOD
POEMS

Skeletal Lights From Afar
FORREST ROTH
FLASH FICTION/PROSE POEMS

That Blue Trickster Time
AMY UYEMATSU
POEMS

2021

Pyre
MAUREEN ALSOP
POEMS

What Falls Away Is Always
KATHARINE HAAKE &

GAIL WRONSKY, EDITORS
ESSAYS

*The Eight Mile
Suspended Carnival*
REBECCA KUDER
NOVEL

Game
M.L. WILLIAMS
POEMS

2020

No, Don't
ELENA KARINA BYRNE
POEMS

One Strange Country
STELLA HAYES
POEMS

*Remembering Dismembrance:
A Critical Compendium*
DANIEL TAKESHI KRAUSE
NOVEL

Keeping Tahoe Blue
ANDREW TONKAVICH
STORIES

2019

Time Crunch
CATHY COLMAN
POEMS

Whole Night Through
L.I. HENLEY
POEMS

Echo Under Story
KATHERINE SILVER
NOVEL

Decoding Sparrows
MARIANO ZARO
POEMS

2012

The Mermaid at the Americana Arms Motel
A.W. DEANNUNTIS
NOVEL

The Time of Quarantine
KATHARINE HAAKE
NOVEL

Frottage & Even As We Speak
MONA HOUGHTON
NOVELLAS

West of Eden:
A Life in 21ˢᵗ Century Los Angeles
CHUCK ROSENTHAL
MAGIC JOURNALISM

2010

Master Siger's Dream
A.W. DEANNUNTIS
NOVEL

Other Countries
RAMÓN GARCÍA
POEMS

A Giant Claw
GRONK
ESSAY BY GAIL WRONSKY
SPANISH TRANSLATION
BY ALICIA PARTNOY
ART

Coyote O'Donohughe's
History of Texas
CHUCK ROSENTHAL
NOVEL

So Quick Bright Things
GAIL WRONSKY
BILINGUAL, SPANISH TRANSLATION
BY ALICIA PARTNOY
POEMS

2009

Bling & Fringe
(The L.A. Poems)
MOLLY BENDALL &
GAIL WRONSKY
POEMS

April, May, and So On
FRANÇOIS CAMOIN
STORIES

One of Those Russian Novels
KEVIN CANTWELL
POEMS

The Origin of Stars
& Other Stories
KATHARINE HAAKE
STORIES

Lizard Dream
KAREN KEVORKIAN
POEMS

Are We Not There Yet?
Travels in Nepal,
North India, and Bhutan
CHUCK ROSENTHAL
MAGIC JOURNALISM

WHAT
BOOKS
PRESS

LOS ANGELES

.